CREAM AND BREAD

BY
JANET MARTIN and ALLEN TODNEM

Illustrated By
ALLEN TODNEM

REDBIRD PRODUCTIONS
Box 363
Hastings, MN. 55033

REDBIRD PRODUCTIONS
Box 363
Hastings, MN. 55033

This book is dedicated to anyone who has ever eaten Cream and Bread.

ACKNOWLEDGEMENTS

Mange Tusen Tak!

— To Andrea Syltie and Farid Saed for their photography work on the book cover.

— To Eunice Pearson and Angie Rose for editing.

— To our families and friends for support ideas and encouragement.

— To our parents for serving CREAM and BREAD.

Preface

As we Americans become more and more a part of the melting pot, we find that we are gradually losing much of the ethnic heritage we so fondly remember. So—just like the hearty suppertime concoction of rich cream and brown sugar on freshly baked bread[1] that we enjoyed in the '40's and 50's, this book is our savory concoction of reminiscences of those by-gone days in rural Scandinavian homes with our Scandinavian Lutheran traditions.

The book is divided into two parts: Part I — Cream — deals with the fun, sometimes foolish, stories and traditions that to our memories are indeed the "cream of the crop." Though we cherish them, we can still sit back and have a good laugh at their expense. Part II — Bread — is literally the meat and potatoes scene with lefse, lutefisk, unforgettable church suppers, and, of course, that wonderful cream and bread dish. As King Harold said to Grandpa, "This is mighty good stuff!"

[1]Some used other toppings such as Karo syrup or chokecherry jelly.

CONTENTS

PART I — CREAM

PART II — BREAD

Part One

CHAPTER 1
THE DIARY OF LARS OLSON

Keep it to yourself,
It isn't that bad.
No one should know if
You're happy or sad.

THE DIARY OF LARS OLSON

For centuries scholars and historians have been pondering the age old question, "What makes a Norwegian grin and bear it?" Since Norwegians aren't the type of people that "let it all hang out," nobody knows much about them at all! But in the late 40's, some light was finally shed on the subject. Someone found Lars Olson's diary! There hadn't been such excitement about finding a piece of Norwegian literature since the discovery of the Viking Runestone in Kensington, Minnesota! Although only a couple of pages were found, serious students of Norwegian history are still busy digging around the barn on the Lars Olson farm to see if maybe they can find more. The following is the complete diary of Lars Olson:

9 January Boy, it's cold. The pastor said in his sermon that it would be good if people wrote down their thoughts. It would get them to think more. I wonder what he meant by that? Since I can't think of anything more to write, I guess there's no sense writing any more today.

16 January Not much has happened since last time I wrote. It's still cold and besides we had 8 more inches of snow this week. Some say it might be a late spring. Ole Rasmussen came over to visit on Tuesday. He didn't have much to say. Lars Pederson's cow froze to death on Thursday. I suppose he'll get a new one.

23 January My how time flies. We had a good sermon today. There was a real bad storm yesterday. Ole Rasmussen had more bad luck. They say his son is going to marry a Catholic. I suppose she will turn if she isn't too stubborn. You can never tell. Mabel said that there was some in church that needed to hear what the Pastor said. I wonder who she was thinking about. She never said.

30 January It was 30 below this week. My it was cold. It was 15 degrees colder than last week. Mabel said she has never seen it so cold, but I think it has been that cold before. I never said anything though.

6 February Thank goodness it is not as cold this week as it was last week. Mabel had some ladies in to organize a doings for Ole Rasmussen's son. Even if he is going to marry a Catholic, some say they should give her a shower in the Lutheran Church since Ole and his wife are members in good standing and Ole's grandfather was a charter member of the church.

13 February We didn't make it to church today because of the weather. I wonder if it will ever quit snowing.

20 February I went to town on Friday. It finally quit snowing. Lars Pederson bought a new manure spreader. I wonder if he ever got a new cow? He didn't say. Lars and I ate dinner at Myrtle's Cafe. We couldn't even get a little roast beef dinner. All she had was fish and three kinds of pie. I suppose it was for the Catholic trade. She won't have any business left if she acts like that.

27 February Mabel says I have to eat early dinner on Thursday. I suppose, I said. She has to serve Ladies Aid in the afternoon. I might as well clean up and go to town then. We've had enough snow for awhile.

5 March The weather has been pretty good this week. I think we can get in the fields early this spring if it stays decent like this. Mabel had some ladies in to plan a doings for Per and his wife. I don't know why there is such fussing about lunch. If each one would make 3 or 4 dozen open faced sandwiches, bring a jar of pickles and a cake it would be all settled.

12 March There was a new family in church today. They sure didn't look Norwegian. The Mrs. had real dark hair. Mabel was a little suspicious of them. Ole's wife said they work in town and don't own any property. I hope they are not hoodlums.

19 March A lady was here for the U. S. census. All those questions. It was none of her business to talk about all that. Ole said he didn't answer her questions either. She even got stuck in my driveway. She should know better than to come out in weather like this.

26 March We had the doings for Per and his wife. It was their 25th wedding anniversary. Per looked mighty uncomfortable with his suit and tie on. He couldn't even roll up his sleeves all afternoon. Good thing it wasn't so hot out. All that fussing for nothing.

2 April Next week I will be in the fields so I will quit this writing for awhile. The weather has held up pretty good this week.

7 November Well we got the grain up and it wasn't a real good year. The hired man took off right during harvest. It's hard to find good help now a days. Some say Ole Jensen is selling out and moving his house to town. I wonder what he'll do in town anyway? I suppose the Mrs. wants to move to town.

14 November I think winter will be early this year. It snowed 5 inches this week. John Johnson's father-in-law's sister died this week. Mabel served her funeral even though she never really did join the church. They say it was old age.

21 November We had the Fall Harvest Festival at church. Mabel has been fussing and stewing all week. We had such a good dinner, I just about told her.

28 November The Pastor spoke on giving money to-day. I think he should wait on that sermon until after the church report is out. He doesn't have to worry about money with everyone bringing him chickens and eggs and everything.

5 December They had a doings in church this week. It was cold outside too. One of the big shots was down to speak. He had us grinning, nodding, and shaking hands right in church. Per Johnson's wife was even laughing out loud. I don't like loud women. He thinks we need a new hymnal. What in the world would we do with the old ones? They're perfectly good. I think he should keep his new fangled ideas to himself and keep his nose out of our business.

12 December Mabel says we got to get a tree. I wonder why she's always in such a rush. She's so busy baking and fussing I don't know why she's thinking of that too. Especially with the way the weather is.

19 December We got our tree yesterday. Martin Olson died yesterday. It was real cold too. Some said they thought he would last till Christmas, but he didn't. Mabel says Johnson's Hardware has new pressure cookers. If she has one of them, I wonder what she'd do with all her spare time.

27 December We had real good lutefisk for Christmas. We've had alot of company, but no new news. The church annual report is out. Mabel says the Rasmussen's could have been a little bit more generous since their son married a Catholic and the church gave her a shower and everything. I wonder how long winter will last anyway.

Footnote: Lars died and was buried in the church cemetery next to the church. The Ladies Aid served a big lunch. There must have been at least 200 people there. Mabel moved to town. Since Lars was the type of person that wouldn't have wanted anyone to read his diary, it would be good not to talk much about it. At least not until after Mabel is dead.

Footnote to the footnote: Since the last footnote was written, Mabel died and was buried right next to Lars in the church cemetery. Some said that Mabel never knew about the diary, so it was a good thing people never talked much about it.

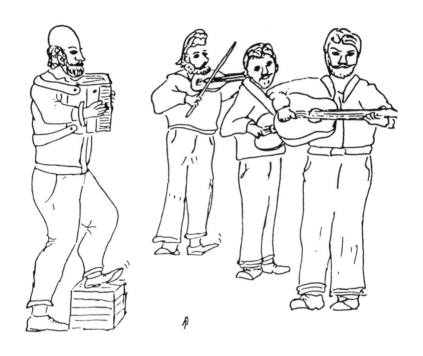

CHAPTER 2
STRINGBANDS ARE FOREVER

The band was in practice,
The kids were upstairs,
The ladies all sat on
The dining room chairs.

The music got louder,
The ladies did too.
The kids were all howling,
So what else was new?

STRING BANDS ARE FOREVER

Many childhood days were spent listening to Father practice his mandoline and sing songs from the black hymnal. He belonged to a group at a church that was referred to as the "string band." Now this was not just any old group — these guys were good! There was Uncle Joe on the guitar, Father on the mandolin, Ben pumping the accordian, and Cliff picking the folk guitar. And any singers who wished to join in were welcomed.

Practice was always held in homes, and that meant we could all go along for the "lunch" that was provided after practice. The men would be in the living room, the ladies would gather in the kitchen to prepare the food, and we kids would be in a bedroom either using the bed as a trampoline or playing our two favorite games: "You Can't Touch the Floor" tag where up to fifteen kids would jump from the dresser to the chair to the bed and then start all over again — and Blind Man's Bluff. — To make sure the "blind man" couldn't see, we'd get a necktie from the closet, tie it around his eyes, and then turn out the lights. One particular night he managed to grope his way into the hall, but then he rolled down the stairs and landed in the living room just as the band was in the midst of the rousing, "When the Roll is Called Up Yonder, I'll be There." The tumble just knocked the wind out of him, but as he lay there so still, we were certain that this was the night God had called the roll for him!

Uncle Joe gave us a good lecture about behaving at string band practice, but even afterward the men chuckled a bit whenever they played that song. The band has long since disbanded, but our memories of that night's fun, horror, and great relief remain forever fresh.

CHAPTER 3
BEAT THE PLATE

The ladies in front
Are craning their necks,
To see how fast
I can write out this check!

BEAT THE PLATE

In Norway, taxes support the state church, so to Midwestern Norwegian Lutherans in the '20's, weekly Sunday offerings were unknown. Church was not even held weekly in some areas, so the Board of Trustees would meet once a year and arbitrarily assess each family a lump sum to pay to the church. Then if the pastor's salary still came up a little short, the Trustees would go out and collect two more dollars from each family. It wasn't until the '30's that offering plates were passed, and then it was done only three times a year — Christmas, Easter, and Pentecost. By the '40's, however, weekly offering envelopes for each family were in vogue. This made it easier for the pastor to account for donations, but no one thought it would be a problem for some of the faithful.

In the rush to get the chores done, breakfast made, table cleared, dishes washed, kids dressed, potatoes peeled for dinner, it was hard to have your offering envelope ready before the service began. So — when do you take the checkbook out, write a check, tear it out, fold it, put it into the envelope, and lick it shut? The pastor was certain to notice if your eyes shifted elsewhere during his sermon. If you counted on a crescendo from the choir, it was sure to be over by the time you were ready to tear out the check. If you waited until the ushers started to the front to get the plates from the altar, you were a goner. The person next to you in the pew would keep holding it out for you to take, and someone would always whisper, "She didn't beat the plate." Uff da mig! Maybe the pastor would settle for a couple of plump frying chickens next week.

CHAPTER 4
SATURDAY NIGHT ALIVE!

The town was alive
With kids on the street
Running fast as they could
Past the judgment seat!

SATURDAY NIGHT ALIVE!

Winter was just a memory. The field planting was finally over. The lilacs were in full bloom, and school was recessed for the next three months. V.B.S. (Vacation Bible School) under the capable leadership of Mrs. Ole Olson, was in full operation. The migrant workers had arrived, and it was summer! It was time for the shops in all the small Midwestern towns to open their doors on Saturday night. It was Saturday Night Alive!

Every Saturday night between Decoration Day[1] and Labor Day[2], the country people would "go to town." By 6:30 on Saturday night, the family was all cleaned up for their weekly visit. All the way to town, Mother, in her clean housedress, threatened the children, "Don't act like a bunch of wild Indians." But little girls in rag curls and pink spoolies, and little boys with clean ears and fresh heinies let Mother's threats go in one ear and out the other. For as soon as the car was parked in town and the last threat given, the country kids were on the loose! They tore around from one store to the next carefully purchasing candy and goodies with their nickels and dimes. They had never felt so much freedom — except at the county fair. For two hours every week they got to do what the lucky town kids took for granted — fun things like tearing down a dark alley, getting a glimpse of the sinners in the

[1]Decoration Day — A day to honor the dead by having programs and clean cemeteries. It also signaled the time of year it was appropriate to wear white shoes.

[2]Labor Day — A day of leisure for town folks who never worked on Saturday anyway. It also signaled the time of year to put away the white shoes.

pool hall[3], looking through comic books at the drug store, and buying a cherry coke and having it served.

Saturday night was a time for mothers to trade at the local stores. If the cream checks[4] were good, the boxed-up groceries would contain such exotic treats as store-bought cookies or bakery bread. They also had a chance to visit with their neighbors. Many towns kept the children occupied with movies so mothers didn't have to worry about them.

The men tended to their banking duties, talked about the crops, and reviewed the temperatures and relative humidity of the previous week. If they were really in deep conversation, the kids knew it was a prime time to get an extra nickel or dime from Dad.

The people, as the saying goes, "came out of the woodwork" on Saturday night. Old men spitting Copenhagen lined the sidewalk benches and reminisced about the war, weather, and other timely topics. And the self-appointed Court of Justice showed up too!

Every small town had one that usually consisted of from two to four blue-haired ladies (usually spinsters and widows of the Lutheran or Baptist persuasion) who took premium parking spots[5] in front of busy respectable businesses. They were dressed fit to kill! Their faces were

[3]Pool hall — This was also known as "the den of the devil."
[4]Cream checks — This means just what it says — checks for cream.

[5]Premium parking spot — These were taken no later than 2:00 P.M.

caked with Lady Esther powder, and the sweet aroma of Evening in Paris drifted out of their car. They neither shopped nor mingled; they just sat. The only reason they were there was to discuss, comment on, and judge everyone who walked in front of the car. Any sin a person had committed (known or unknown) was brought to light. Targets of their acid tongues were people like Handbag Hannah,[6] floozies with red lips and low cut dresses, and anyone they assumed had hard liquor on his breath or sen-sen in his pocket.

Teenagers, another prime target, were oblivious to the Court of Justice. They didn't even know these ladies existed. They were too busy spending their time in the show house or cruising the three block long main street. They didn't even care about the real calling card of the night — the jackpot![7]

At 8:30 or 9:00 P.M. (depending upon the town), the sirens would go off, and people would flock to hear the winners of the jackpot. This was also the only time in the evening that the Court of Justice left their cars. After

---

[6]Handbag Hannah — A bag lady.

[7]Jackpot — This was usually worth about $25 in trade at a local store. It was said that Thelma Peterson's grandmother (See Chapter 9) heard the siren for the jackpot go off right during a wedding. She automatically jumped up to leave, but the ushers told her to sit down, so she did. It wasn't the siren after all; it was just loud wedding bells!

the drawing, the respectable people cleared out of town in twenty minutes flat, and the stores were closed. Even though the kids caught heck all the way home, they didn't care. They knew that come next Saturday that wonderful time would be repeated. It would be Saturday Night Alive! once again.

CHAPTER 5
UFF DA, ISH DA, FY DA, SHUCKS

Out of money,
Out of luck,
Uff da, Ish da,
Fy da, Shucks!

UFF DA, ISH DA, FY DA, SHUCKS

Most American born Norwegians have adjusted to the fact that English — not Norwegian — is the mother tongue in the United States. Since the Norskies are known as a stubborn people who are not easily persuaded, this switch from speaking Norwegian to English was slow and gradual. (Some say it took four generations). But after the big war (WWII), it was almost complete! A big majority of the Norwegians still can't pronounce words such as "thousand" (tousand) or "jello" (yellow), but nevertheless they can and do make themselves understood (if you can get them to talk).

Since the Norskies spoke Norwegian in the United States for over one hundred years, it stands to reason that some of their words just wouldn't die — three of them especially: uff da, ish da and fy da. Not only did these three words survive, they have been assimilated into the English language. Webster never has and probably never will list them as proper words, but everyone uses them. However, because your average Italian, business, preacher, and doctor doesn't understand the subtle differences in their meanings, uff da, ish da, and fy da have become the most abused words in the English language.[1]

So, for your clarification, here are situations when it is proper to use them. From these you can easily determine their definitions.

[1]We did a survey to back up this fact.

AN UFF DA SITUATION:

The Mrs. carefully gathers up a bucketful of watermelon rinds left over from the family reunion picnic. The next morning she's up before the chickens and before the flies get thick, making watermelon pickles. After canning forty-two pints, she finds that six of the jars didn't seal, and they are the ones she is planning to enter in Open Class at the county fair. Now she's in a pickle! And she grumbles, "Uff dá, uff da!"

A FY DA SITUATION:

A floozy who wears gaudy jewelry, fiery-red lipstick, dark-seamed nylons, and dresses with low necklines (lower than the jewelry neckline) and short skirts — moves into town and rents. What's more, she's divorced and doesn't have any known relatives in the area. She's loud and opinionated, and the first week she's spotted playing bingo for money while her kids don't have decent shoes to wear to church. Fy da, fy da!

AN ISH DA SITUATION:

The hired man steps into a cow pile, then walks into your kitchen, sits down, and asks for a cold drink of water and a cookie. (If it's cold outside he might ask for a cup of coffee with a sugar lump.) You've just washed and waxed the floor, but he doesn't notice it. He has Copenhagen running down his chin and shirt. Some of his teeth are missing; the ones left are brown. He looks awful and smells worse. After he leaves, you mutter, "Ish da, ish da!"

SHUCKS!

We include this word because it was rumored that some Norwegian immigrants were saying it on the boats. Since its meaning is so similar to uff da, if you feel more comfortable using it instead of the pure expression, go ahead!

CHAPTER 6
YOU'LL LIVE — IT WILL HEAL

The kettle is whistling,
The towel is in place,
The kid is a-hollerin',
"It's scalding my face!"

YOU'LL LIVE — IT WILL HEAL

People bragged about their healthy kids and very seldom took them to a doctor unless they seemed nigh unto death! Lopping around the house for two weeks with one kind of ailment or another was not uncommon. "You'll live — it will heal," was a phrase we often heard.

The following were Mrs. Ole Risetter's tried and true remedies for some common maladies:

FLU   Let the kids stay home from school if temperature is above 102 degrees. I've never heard of anyone dying from it.

TONSILITIS   Give ice cream. If it's bad, get a shot in the butt.

TONSILLECTOMY   Give a popsicle along with ice cream. Let kids rest in bed until they get mean and ornery. That's a sure sign they are getting better.

COLD   It will run its course.

CHEST COLD   Massage Vicks into chest and top with wool rag pinned to pajama top.

COUGHING AT NIGHT   Rinse rag in very cold water, wring out, and wrap around neck. Put dry rag on top. Fasten both with safety pins.

PNEUMONIA If spitting up blood, throw dish-
    towel over head and lean over whistling tea
    kettle. If chest doesn't loosen, call doctor
    over to house.

DIARRHEA Eat milk toast. This is also good for
    other things.

RINGWORM If on body, swab with Hilex. If on
    head, shave it and put on skull cap. Stay
    out of barns and away from kids who have it.

SORE EYES Wipe with boric acid solution.

WHOOPING COUGH The noise will scare the devil
    out of you, so see a doctor.

BLOOD POISONING When the streaks start to move
    up, see a doctor.

TETANUS Get a shot then.

COLIC Put Karo syrup in milk. Let the baby cry it out
    so he doesn't get spoiled.

PREGNANCY Loose dresses will keep it under wraps
    for eight months.

CANKER SORES Alum is good. Stay away from
    oranges.

TOOTHACHE Use cloves and a hot water bottle at
    night. Otherwise, grin and bear it.

SORE Dab on mercurochrome or iodine.

INFECTION Soak in epsom salts, then put on mus-
    tard poltice mixture to draw it out. It will heal.

CONSTIPATION Castor oil, prunes, or raisins are good. Kids will often try to hide condition because they dread enemas.

DEPRESSION Try a kick in the seat. Hard work never killed anyone.

SORE THROAT Drink hot lemonade with honey. (Watkins lemon nectar will do in a pinch). Paint thoroughly with tincture of merthiolate.

HIVES Cut out the strawberries.

CHICKEN POX Try a baking soda bath. Oatmeal can be used too. Since it's good to get it over with, expose other children in the house and invite the neighbor kids in.

MEASLES Try to determine if they are three day or hard measles. If they are the hard ones, keep quiet, pull down the shades, and wear sunglasses.

WARTS Swab with vinegar. Wrap white adhesive tape around them for six days, and they might fall off.

Keep a can of carbo salve and a hot water bottle on hand at all times. Then rely on common sense.

If Mrs. Ole Risetter forgot any remedies you can add your own by filling in the blanks.

_____

_____

_____

_____

_____

CHAPTER 7
THE WRITTEN WORD

The paper was read,
The news was not new;
I knew all the names
Except for a few!

THE WRITTEN RECORD

There was life after the Decorah-Posten! Before computers, heavy reliance on television, and Watergate — news was usually transferred via eight-party telephone lines and then documented in the local newspaper. Nearly every settlement with fifty people recorded the weekly doings of its citizens in papers with such cosmopolitan names as the *Herald*, *Tribune*, and *Times*.

Contributing editors were local Rona Barrett's from various townships and villages who had access to the really pertinent information: who had coffee with whom and when, who visited with whom on Sunday afternoon, and who had company from out of town. A favorite line to sum up each socializing was, "A good time was had by all."

Births, deaths, and weddings were recorded in style! A wedding was generally a two-column splash brimming over with the fascinating details that favorite Aunts Inga and Ellie poured coffee at the reception, Cousin Minnie sang a beautiful rendition of "O Promise Me," and Martha Solie from down the street had lent the bride her fingertip veil.

On the front page we dutifully read about seed time, harvest and pest infestations as we followed with interest the plight and progress of the farmer. Storms were also front page stories, and big ones brought out local reactions and observations. Even the more mundane relative humidity and temperature statistics were recorded and remembered for years.

The local paper also kept us abreast of church, school, and community activities. It even kept juvenile delinquency to a minimum! Woe unto any kid who found his name in the court news! Even though we regularly complained, "There wasn't much in there this week,"[1] we preferred it to the Reader's Digest two to one.

The only thing that really gave the local paper a run for its money was the church annual report!

When that came out, all pretenses of righteousness went out the window! In the back of the report, all the members' names were listed along with how much money each had given to the church that year. And, oh, there were some surprises! Those pages were the object of much study and discussion!

Magazines were popular too. *Life*, the *Saturday Evening Post*, and *National Geographic*[2] kept us in touch with the rest of the world. Most farm families also subscribed to three or four different farm magazines that contained up-to-date farming articles for the Mr., recipes for the Mrs., and puzzles for the kids.

[1]The editor must have felt like Moses. The people always expected miracles.

[2]National Geographic — This international magazine filled with pictures of half-naked heathens was the closest thing to pornography that came into our homes.

CHAPTER 8
HOUSECLEANING

It happened in spring,
It happened in fall,
The lady of the house,
She went through it all.

HOUSECLEANING

Just as the farmer had a time to plant and a time to harvest, the Scandinavian housewife[1] had a time to clean and a time to really clean! Since cleanliness was next to godliness (even the mouth got washed out if it was dirty), she went about her housecleaning duties with such conviction and fervor that nothing short of a disaster could stop her. From Monday through Saturday, sun-up to sundown (and sometimes a little longer), she cleaned with full steam. She never sat. She was in perpetual motion. If "idle hands were a tool of the devil," the diligent Scandinavian housewife didn't have to worry. Leisure time was not part of her schedule. It was as out of place to her as banker's hours.[2]

The cleaning schedule was as unalterable as the Hardanger Fjord. There was weekly cleaning, spring housecleaning, fall housecleaning, and pre-Yule cleaning.

[1]We know the Norwegian and Swedish women cleaned all the time. We are not sure, however, if the Finnish and Danish women did the same. If you want to find out, ask someone who is either Finnish or Danish. They probably could tell you. We didn't ask because we don't know anyone who is Finnish or Danish (outside of Mrs. Jensen, and she's dead now), and this isn't the type of question you ask a total stranger. Some say Mrs. Jensen let her dog sleep in her kitchen. Fy da!

[2]Banker's hours — This was a slang term used for people who worked only eight hours a day from Monday through Friday and only a half day on Saturday.

WEEKLY CLEANING

This was done according to Hoyle — that is, there was a right way and a right time to clean. The Scandinavian housewife in Iowa had the same cleaning schedule as her counterpart in northern Minnesota. Why, everyone knew that a person washed on Monday and ironed on Tuesday. Dish towels were even stamped and embroidered to validate this fact.

The work week began with the wash on Monday. Even though some articles of clothing were worn for a week straight, heaven forbid if anyone whould see a gray-tinged wash on the line! Clothes were soaked, boiled, scrubbed, rubbed, washed, rinsed, bleached, and blued. (You couldn't beat a wringer washer for getting things clean.) Then they were hung outside on lines to dry. (It was imperative that everything smell fresh.) Next they were vigorously sprinkled with water, wrapped up tight, covered good, and put to rest for the night. In the morning they were ready for the iron or mangle. Besides, it was Tuesday, the day to iron.

The work week was finished on Saturday night.[3] After the children had had their weekly baths and the jello had been set for Sunday dining, there was only one thing left to clean — the kitchen floor. (The slop pail was usually emptied at this time too.) The housewife got on her hands and knees and scrubbed. (How could you get a

[3]We decided not to go through the whole work-week schedule. It would take a whole week to write about it and would greatly increase the price of this book.

floor really clean if you used a mop? That just wouldn't get the corners good.) Then she waxed the floor to a spit polish shine. After the wax dried (about thirty to forty minutes), newspapers were put all over the floor to save and protect it from whatever dirt or dust might get tracked in. The papers were picked up on Sunday morning and clean rag rugs laid down. Tomorrow would be Monday; time to do the wash once again.

SPRING HOUSECLEANING

Sometime between the vernal equinox and Easter, the Scandinavian housewife was infected with Spring Housecleaning Fever, a malady[4] that struck for three to four weeks every spring and was as contagious as a new molasses bar recipe. During this time, all the stops were pulled out. Everything was turned upside down, inside out, and then put right side up and right side out again. Spring housecleaning was as powerful as a strong North Sea wind.

Dishes and silver pieces that were used only for special occasions — the silver wedding anniversaries and Confirmations — were taken out of storage, washed and polished, and put right back in place again. Old shelf paper was discarded, and new was put in. Rugs were wisked off the floor, put on the clothes line, and royally beaten. (There was a special utensil used for this beating process.) Clothes were cleared out of closets and taken

---

[4]Some authorities say this malady might have been a virus.

out of drawers. They were shaken out, hung on the line to freshen, then brought back in, put in mothballs, and laid to rest until Fall. Nightgowns that were being saved for the time you might have to go to the hospital were not spared the treatment either. And woe to any spiders and their webs because walls and ceilings were scrubbed down good! Storm windows were taken off, and once again fresh breezes filled the rooms. Curtains were washed, pressed, stretched, and starched. After all the work was done and the house had passed the white glove test, the malady subsided, and eveything returned to normal.

FALL HOUSECLEANING

Summer brought a slack time in housecleaning activities, but this was just the calm before the storm! After the harvest was in, the canning done, and the church fall festival completed,[5] Fall Housecleaning Syndrome set in. Everything was again turned upside down, scrubbed, rubbed, washed, and cleaned! And in three to four weeks, the affliction had run its course.

[5]A lot of people enjoyed watching Lawrence Welk at this time of the year.

PRE-YULE CLEANING

Pre-Yule cleaning was certainly not as intense as spring and fall housecleaning, but it was the final good cleaning of the calendar year. The corners received extra attention, and the furniture got the once over, once again. Baking was at its zenith with julekake, flatbrod, and dozens of fattigmand, rosettes, krumkake, and sandbakkelse being stored away for the family's Christmas and all the drop-in company that the season would bring.

Approximately seventy-five to eighty days after Christmas, spring housecleaning would again return. The cleaning cycle, like seedtime and harvest, went on.

CHAPTER 9
HOW TO DO A DOINGS

Behind the scenes
The work is done,
It isn't always
Games and fun.

HOW TO DO A DOINGS

Prelude: There were always many doings to plan — Luther League banquets, showers, family reunions, and silver wedding anniversaries — to name just a few. This poem tells how to do a wedding shower.

The phone was ringing with that "ding it" loud bell.
Mrs. Olson[1] was on with some good news to tell.
The secret was out, my hunches[2] proved right —
Ola asked Thelma for her hand last night.

The stage was all set, the ground work was laid;
Now plans for the shower had to be made!
The date fixed for May, three weeks from tonight
In the church basement, the usual site.

All met at Olson's and made out the list;
Oh goodness gracious, we hoped none were missed.
We sent out the cards to friends in the city;
We gave them the facts, and signed — "The
     Committee."

[1]Mrs. Olson was a big buxom busybody with a heart of gold who always knew the news first. Emil, her husband, never got a word in edge-wise.

[2]Hunches — Mrs. Olson had told us that way back when Ola was eighteen years old, he had written the following verse in Thelma's autograph book: "Roses are red, violets are blue, sugar is sweet, and so are you." So we thought they would get married someday.

The program was planned; we knew all along
That Betty would sing that cute little song.
Della would read with her big booming voice.
She always was talking; we had no real choice.

Arranging the lunch was always a worry.
Who would bring what put all in a flurry:
There were nuts and mints and pickles to bring.
We must not forget and leave out a thing!

Three of the ladies would bake all the bread (buns)
And bring the minced ham[3] to use as the spread.
Some would have cookies and nut bars to bake
And Myrtle would bring a beautiful cake. (And a jello)

Just one thing remained for them to decide:
What gift would the committee buy for the bride?
Something she needed would be very nice.
Something to use for the rest of her life.

Postlude: The committee decided to get Thelma a good sturdy black frying pan and an ironing board for a shower gift. Thelma's aunt, Bertha Tronson, the one who would pour coffee at the wedding, had already bought her an iron. The shower went off without a hitch. There was plenty of food. Mrs. Hjalmer O. Rud won a new chore boy for being the lady who could make the most words out of "Wedding Bells" in twenty minutes. Mrs.

[3]The recipe for minced ham is found in the chapter entitled. "Grandma's Favorites." Spam could be substituted.

Peter Peterson, Thelma's future father-in-law's sister, found the masking tape under her plate and won the door prize — a new dish rag. (She's been real lucky lately. She won two cakes on the cake walk at the school carnival last week, and her son-in-law won the jackpot[4] at the drawing in town last Saturday night.) Thelma thanked everyone — especially the committee who had worked so long and hard. A good time was had by all!

As long as we're talking about the shower, maybe a few words about the wedding of Mr. and Mrs. Ola Johnson might be in order then. The now Mrs. Ola Johnson (nee Thelma Peterson) was a beautiful blushing bride. Ola was nervous when he said, "I do," but everyone could hear him. At least those of us who sat in the front rows could. Ingrid, the flower girl, (Bertha Tronson's granddaughter) put up a fuss and said she wasn't going to walk down the aisle. But Bertha promised her a Dixie Cup if she would do it. She did it. As usual, no one breathed when Pastor O. A. Knudson said, "If there is any reason why these two should not be joined together, let him say so now or forever hold his peace." But nobody said anything. After a short trip to Duluth and the North Shore, Mr. and Mrs. Ola Johnson are at home. He is engaged in farming with his father. They say she can roll out a pie crust just like her mother.

[4]Jackpot — See the chapter entitled, "Saturday Night Alive!"

CHAPTER 10
REFLECTIONS ON SILVERS

The table was set;
The cloth was white lace;
The nuts and the mints
Were all in their place.

The coffee was brewing,
The readings were good.
The six "turned out"
As we prayed they would.

REFLECTIONS ON SILVERS

Right up there with Reformation Sunday stood the Silver Wedding Anniversary! This was a celebration for longstanding members of the congregation who had been married only once and to the same person for twenty-five years. It was a time for uncles, aunts, cousins, and friends to rejoice in the church basement on a Sunday afternoon.

The children "put on" the celebration, but the real work was done by the ladies of the Aid who painstakingly arranged the details well in advance of the day. The cake was usually a bakery cake, second to none, with silver bells and the number 25 glistening on top. The corsages matched the trim on the frosting and the mints. Open-faced sandwiches (usually egg salad or minced ham), jello, bars, pickles, and punch made for a good afternoon lunch.

The Mr. hated to be there. This was his time to nap. Besides, all this fussing made him feel a little foolish. But the Mrs. loved it! It was her time to shine![1] After all, she had brought many pans of bars for other silver celebrations, and to think that her children all "turned out!"[2] Sometimes the Mrs. even wore her wedding dress for the grand occasion. If, after six children and all those years she could still squeeze into it (that is, with the help of her

[1] She felt just like "Queen for a Day."
[2] If your children turned out, it meant (a) they did not marry out of the faith, and (b) the local newspaper never had to print their names in the court news.

good girdle), she was entitled to wear it. Usually though, she just bought herself a new dress and got a new permanent for the pictures.

The program was the highlight — at least for the adults! Songs were sung and stories were told. Some we had heard time and time again, but we always laughed and clapped heartily anyway. The grandchildren played their piano pieces. And there were the readings! Those were the clever little poems, essays, and stories on marriage found in farm periodicals, "The Lutheran Herald," and "Ideals."

For the kids, the nuts and mints made the day! Outside of weddings which they rarely got to attend, silver wedding anniversaries were the only time they had free access to them. And other than an occasional dirty look from the lady pouring coffee at the end of the table, it was clear sailing! The nuts and mints were wiped clean before the coffee pots were passed around for the second time. Then the kids started on the sugar lumps!

And, oh my, the gifts! There were silver trays and silver bowls, and all those crisp new dollar bills tucked in the cards! "How could they ever thank everyone?" the Mrs. commented as the Kodak s were snapping.

When it was over, the Aid cleaned up the kitchen, took home the dish towels to wash, and were out of church by 5 P.M. They had to get home to start supper. Besides, the men had chores to do.

CHAPTER 11
AS SIMPLE AS BLACK AND WHITE

Black is black
White is white:
They were wrong —
We were right!

AS SIMPLE AS BLACK AND WHITE

There once were some Vikings of old
Who went out looking for gold;
They landed on sand
Which is now Ireland,
And the races were mixed, so I'm told.

— *Author Unknown*

History tells of the Norwegian and Irish interacting as far back as the eighth century when the Viking sea rovers ravaged the coasts of Europe. But in the Midwest in the '50's, Norse and Irish mingling just never caught on! We were Lutherans, and they were Catholics — for time and all eternity! And we were told that their eternity and ours would surely be spent in different places! When Martin Luther Olson fell for Margaret Mary McCarthy (we don't know her Confirmation name), we knew without a doubt that he was headed straight for hell! Anyone who would sign over his kids to the Pope, get married in the morning and agree to a wild wedding dance, had surely given up his inheritance in the Kingdom!

But those Irish were lucky though! They could wear lipstick, play bingo and cards in church, go to dances, shoot pool — and erase it all in a ten minute session with Father O'Malley in a curtained booth. They didn't even have any sacred two-hour Saturday morning Confirmation classes to attend. But every sunny Saturday they'd show up right outside First Lutheran and get up a ball game. All the while, stern Pastor A. O. Haugen, oblivious to the action and raucous noise, continued to pound Bible history into us until we hoped against hope that our church walls — like those of Jericho — would come a'tumblin' down, and we'd be put out of this misery that was supposd to make us good Christians.

When Fridays came, so did our chance at sweet revenge. The score was easily evened when we'd call them "toe-kissing, mackerel-snappers" while chowing down juicy hot dogs. Lent was also time to give the "minnow-munchers" a little taste of purgatory. Since we knew they were expected to give up something for the season (usually candy), we never hesitated to play the role of the serpent and put them through the same forbidden fruit scene that Adam and Eve experienced. "What did you give up for Lent?" we'd smugly ask as we'd pop a good-sized piece of chocolate into our mouths. Before they could answer, we'd add, "We've never heard of anyone dying from taking just one little bite."

Even though we loved to antagonize them (Why shouldn't we — they never had to wear those stuffy suit-coats, ties, and white shirts to church), we did enjoy their company. By the time we were old enough to date, the forbidden fruit looked even better. But introducing someone to your parents whose last name began with either "O" or "Mc" (a dead give-away) was no easy task. You knew, without a doubt, they'd be as welcome as a major outbreak of wheat rust!

On Sunday afternoons, Mom, Dad, and their ten kids named after saints would pile into three-seater station wagons protected by St. Christopher and drive by your house. But you knew they weren't coming to visit. They were on their way to a Knights of Columbus picnic to play bingo and drink beer.

They drank beer after a funeral too! This was as disgusting a practice as was going to "wake their dead." Anyone respectable would have had a review or visitation at the funeral home with lunch and coffee afterward.

But, nevertheless, home missions flourished as both sides tried to convert the other. A good opportunity came in June when the migrant workers arrived in town. Then it was a race to see which side could get the most migrant children into their own Vacation Bible Schools by offering free rides, balloons, bean feeds, and picnics. But though each side secretly rejoiced when someone "changed" and when one of the "lost was found," brave pioneers such as Martin Luther Olson and Margaret Mary McCarthy paved the way for new and better relationships between the Irish and Norwegians.

> *Irish are Catholics we're told;*
> *Lutherans, they walk streets of gold;*
> *So convert them, my friend,*
> *To a more blessed end,*
> *Before they are dead and go cold.*

We've put all the kidding aside.
For in the Irish we surely take pride;
We're not running a race,
We should all have a place
Up in heaven with God when we die.

LEPRECHAUNS & GNOMES

There are many stories of Ole and Per,
McNeary, O'Halloran, and Rose;
Little people are rare,
In both places they fare;
You're lucky to see one of those.

Leprechauns are the Irish delight,
The Norsemen hold dear their Gnomes;
Whatever your plight
If you see one at night —
Welcome him into your home.

It matters not whether you're peasant or king.
A warm hearth is all that they need.
Good luck they will bring,
That's reason to sing!
Their wisdom you always should heed.

CHAPTER 12
NEIMEN NEIMEN — TIMES ARE CHANGIN'

Eating out,
Night on the town,
Leisure time,
Let your hair down!

NEIMEN NEIMEN — TIMES ARE CHANGIN'

Life changed dramatically after World War II. Pressure cookers were on the scene, and wood cook stoves were becoming passe. A man's best friend was his Dodge Fargo pick-up. Running water was being taken for granted, and indoor toilets were a way of life. Men were wearing short-sleeved shirts to church in the summer, and respectable women were seen wearing peddle pushers in town. Neimen du da! What was this world coming to anyway?

Do you remember when . . .

  . . . "letting it all hang out" had something to do with laundry?

  . . . "getting away from it all" meant visiting relatives on Sunday?

  . . . "fast foods" had to do with cream and bread?

  . . . "eating out" meant either going to the local implement dealer for a pancake feed or going to a church supper?

  . . . "a night on the town" was buying groceries, banking, and visiting friends on Saturday night?

  . . . "R & R" meant read and rest on Sunday afternoon?

  . . . "The night life" was plowing after dark?

  . . . "going to lunch with the girls" meant taking dinner to the men in the fields?

. . . "letting your hair down" meant taking out your spoolies and bobby pins in the morning?

. . . "leisure time" was playing horseshoe at a family reunion or driving around looking at the fields on Sunday afternoons?

. . . "the country club scene" was a phrase used to describe an active 4-H Club?

Part Two

CHAPTER 13
THE LEGEND OF LEFSE

Ole lost his spuds
In the bottom of the sea,
Per made a deal
For the lefse recipe.

THE LEGEND OF LEFSE

Ole Russetson, troll god of mashed potatoes, was in an awful dilemma! It was a life or death matter then!

One day while fishing the fjords for cod, his boat capsized, and all the seed potatoes went to the bottom of the sea. As caretaker of all the seed potatoes for the troll gods, Ole Russetson knew he was in trouble! And this is why it was no joke!

Potatoes were the main ingredient in lefse, and lefse wasn't called "the food of the gods" for nothing. Lefse, eaten three times a day, was the substance that gave Norskie troll gods their ability to stay aloof, to hide their emotions, and to keep calm at all costs. (There was one exception: Thor was the only troll god who wouldn't eat lefse. It showed! That stubborn god thundered around all over acting like a mortal fool.)

Now Ole Russetson felt really bad. How could he have been so foolish as to "put all his potatoes in one basket?" Why hadn't he left some of his seed potatoes on dry land? The troll gods were running out of lefse, and he knew he had to get some potatoes.

Ole had only one way out. He had to break the rules! He did the unthinkable! He contacted a mortal — Per Johnson, a loud, wild, savage Viking potato farmer from Trondheim. Said Ole to Per, "Per, I'm in trouble then! You give me a bushel of seed potatoes, and I'll give you the trolls' secret for staying calm and aloof." Per agreed.

What did he have to lose? He had never seen anyone so in control of himself as Ole Russetson. When Per excitedly gave his wife the lefse recipe, she immediately built a fire. And within two days, the neighbors noticed a difference — Per and his family had changed! They had become aloof, calm, and in control. But nobody could figure out why because Per and his family wouldn't talk about it.

In time, however, Per's wife became lax, and one day she let the cat out of the bag by giving the lefse recipe to the committee putting together a Ladies Aid cookbook for the centennial celebration of their church. The rest is history! The recipe spread across the Norwegian valleys like brush fires! Everyone began eating lefse.

And a real change came over them! They became aloof, calm, and in control. Cleng Peerson[1] decided they needed a new Norway to keep this new breed of Norwegian people pure, so he brought them to the United States. But alas — his dream of an unadulterated community shattered because a few of the weaker transplanted Norwegians broke the rules and married people of other nationalities, In a short time there were all kinds of brown-eyed, dark-haired, thin-armed Norwegians walking around! What's more, things such as tortillas, pizzas, wafers, and other watered-down imitations of lefse began to appear. Then the inevitable happened! The people began to revert back to their old ways: they began to be emotional, to hug in public, to shake hands with total strangers in church.

[1]Cleng Peerson — We're sure you know who he was.

However, all was not lost! There were a few purebreds preserved. You won't find them in any encounter group or clapping their hands in church, but when you hear someone say, "That's nothing to talk about," you know you've found a real live one!

Footnote: The bad news is that in giving the recipe to mortals, poor Ole Russetson was demoted. The good news is that the transplanted Norwegians who remained loyal to Cleng Peerson's dream never knew of Ole Russetson's fate. They bestowed upon him the highest honor they could think of. They named a potato after him. They called it the Russet.

Easy on the flour,
Fast on the pace
Or the dough will stick
All over the place.

Roll 'em out thin,
Fry 'em up quick;
With butter and sugar
They'll go down slick.

POTATO LEFSE

5 c. mashed potates
1½ c. flour
2T. melted butter

1 ts. salt
1 tsp. sugar

Cook potatoes and mash the day before. Mash again before measur-
ing. Makes 12 medium rounds.

HARDANGER LEFSE

2 eggs
2 c. sour cream
½ t. soda
½ c. sugar

pinch of salt
1½ t. ground cardamom (optional)
3¾ c. flour to roll

Put in refrigerator overnight. Go easy on flour as you can always add
more. Take a teaspoon and roll in flour like flatbread. Fry in a pancake griddle a bit on both sides. Store in big container. To serve, put
between damp towels to moisten so they are soft. Then spread with
butter, sugar and cinnamon. Fold over and cut in wedges to serve. A
very old recipe.

(Cont.)
LEFSE

4 c. riced potatoes
1 tsp. salt
¼ c. shortening

¼ c. very rich cream (creamery)
1¼ c. flour

Cook potatoes and rice while hot. Add salt, shortening, and cream. Cool. Just before you roll your lefse, add the flour. A pastry cloth and sleeve work well when you roll it out. Makes 10 to 12.

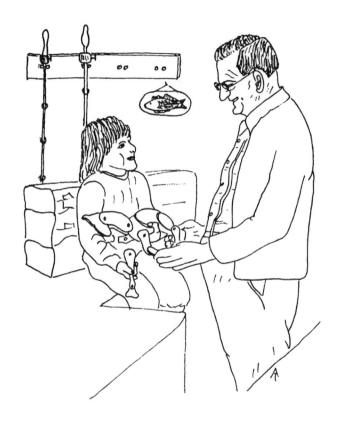

CHAPTER 14
THE LEGEND OF LUTEFISK

Tell me again
That fable of old
How Vikings turned cod
Into Norwegian gold.

THE LEGEND OF LUTEFISK

Early one morning while cod fishing in the fjords, Jens Luteness had an exceptionally big catch. Was he ever lucky! He thought to himself, "I haven't been this lucky since I asked the Mrs. to marry me, and she said, 'You know, Jens, you're not the only fish in the sea, but I'm not getting any younger, so I suppose you'll have to do then.' "

Jens, excited as all get out, hurried home to hang up his catch in the trees to dry. But to his dismay, he discovered that he didn't have enough limbs on his trees to hang up all the fish. Now he had a dilemma! While he was scratching his head trying desperately to figure out where he could dry the rest of the fish, Mrs. Luteness said, "Why don't you just throw the rest of the fish in the rain barrel where I store my used wash water. We'll think of something to do with them after morning coffee. Now, vaer sa god."

When they were just finishing their coffee, their neighbor, Per Johnson, came to visit. They got so busy talking about the weather that Jens plum forgot about his catch.

After many weeks, Jens went out to check the rain barrels. He knew it hadn't rained for forty days, but he wanted to make sure. Then he remembered the fish! "Oh Neimen, ish da," he said to himself. "I'll bet they are all spoiled by now." But little did he know he had stumbled onto something big! Not one fish had rotted! He got so excited he just about started to talk to himself. Instead he called to the Mrs., "Kom hit. I see there is more than one way to skin a fish!" Since wash water was only a combination of birch bark and water,[1] it would be easy to preserve cod fish by the bucketsful! He chuckled, "All I have to do now is figure out how to get rid of the terrible smell."[2]

Now that Jens Luteness had a head on his shoulders! Some say that was why he was elected President of the North Trondelag Association for the Preservation of Cod Fish. He went to work to solve the problems, and quicker than you could say, "Hans Nielsen Hauge," he solved it! He did just what his wife had been doing for years to get the birch bark and water mixture smell out of her clothes. He rinsed them in clean fjord water. It didn't surprise him either when the smell left.

Because of his discovery, the North Trondelag Association for the Preservation of Cod Fish not only named this new preservation process after him (they called it lute fisk), they saw to it that after he was stone dead, he was canonized. And people today still celebrate his find by eating lutefisk by the bucketfuls!

[1]Birch bark and water — This mixture produces, in layman's language, a lye so caustic that it was said that fingernails still grew on the Vikings after they had been dead for years.
[2]Smell — it was stronger than Gumlaost i.e., it stunk to high heaven.

Postscript: For some unknown reasons, heathens, Catholics, and other non-Norwegians have persisted in spreading awful lies and rumors about lutefisk. We agree that the consistency of the fish would make anyone throw up. And even though one might question its food value after looking at it, the real flavor *does not* (as they say) come when it is put on the back porch for dogs to sprinkle. The irony of this whole situation is that non-Norwegians are not only eating lutefisk on the sly, but they're enjoying it too!

CHAPTER 15
"HEY! GUTORMSON'S HAVE A NEW BABY!"
TIME FOR ROMMEGROT

Babies were always a special treat,
'cause people would bring in goodies to eat.
And the greatest treat without a doubt
Was when someone came with Rommegrot!

HEY! GUTORMSON'S HAVE A NEW BABY!
(TIME FOR ROMMEGROT)

Today children ask questions about video games, space missions, high performance automobiles, and nuclear war. We were no less curious, but the times were simpler, and we just asked — Why does water run down hill? How many stars could you wish upon if you ever could get on a star? But one of the greatest mysteries of all to us was why the Gutormson's had so many kids.

Mrs. "G" was an unusually large woman who always wore a flowered dress and worked very hard in the garden. Because of her size and the fullness of her dress, we never knew for sure when the "happening" would take place. Eight kids already lived at home when one Sunday the pastor announced the *new* arrival. We asked Mother why we didn't have nine children in our family. She just said we'd have to be older to understand.

We really didn't mind that answer much because everytime a new baby arrived in the neighborhood, the big kettle was brought up from the basement, put on the stove, and a rich cream pudding called rommegrot would take form once again. We'd sit for hours watching the bubbles burst on the surface and smelling the pleasant aroma that filled the kitchen. It seemed that this was all part of the ritual of having babies.

Once, the milkman came with more than the usual amount of milk and cream, and we thought we had missed the announcements at church completely. But we soon discovered that the special occasion was Christmas, and we were indeed celebrating the birth of a child. It was a very special event, and to this day we get out the kettles for Christmas and start the rommegrot boiling early in the morning.

By the way, the Gutormson's stopped with nine children!

If you haven't tried rommegrot for your special occasions, we have included some delicious recipes taken from the church cookbook of Bethany Lutheran, a rural congregation near Windom, Minnesota.

ROME GROT   Mrs. Helmer (Sylve) Wing

1 c. butter (melted)
1 c. flour (mix smooth)
1 c. buttermilk (cold)
    Bring to boil.

3 c. cold milk
Salt (small amount)

ROMMEGROT

**Mrs. Alvin (Doris) Holmen
Mrs. Ingval (Manda) Ingbritson**

1 pt. thick whipping cream
½ c. flour
½ tsp. salt

2 c. whole milk
2 tsp. sugar or more if you
like it sweeter

Heat cream to boiling point and let boil slowly for about 10 to 15 minutes. Add the flour slowly, stirring constantly. Cook and stir until the butter separates and comes to the top. Pour the butter off and save it to pour on top of rommegrot. Keep doing this until you get the amount of butter you want on top. Then slowly add the 2 cups of milk, beating good after each addition. Let come to a boil. Add your salt and sugar, letting it come to a boil again. Pour into a casserole sprinkling cinnamon and sugar on top. Lastly add the butter you saved for the topping. Serve warm or hot. It may be kept warm in a very low oven. Good luck! Serves 4 to 6.

ROMME GROT (Scandinavian)

**Mrs. Paul
Ingbritson**

1 quart whipping cream (at
least 24 hours old)
1 tsp. salt

1 T. sugar
1 c. flour
1 quart milk (boiled)   (Cont.)

Use heavy kettle, boil cream 10 to 15 minutes. Add flour slowly using a wire whip to keep mixture smooth, keep boiling on lower heat and stirring until butter appears. Add boiled milk and boil and stir to right consistency. Add sugar and salt. Put into bowl and pour butter over. Sprinkle with sugar and cinnamon. Serve lukewarm.

CHAPTER 16
CHURCH SUPPERS

The table was set
With food all in place.
All bow your heads
It's time to sing grace.

CHURCH SUPPERS

The annual fall church supper was a highlight for anyone growing up in the '50's. The supper was usually associated with a speaker who had just spent five years as a missionary in "Darkest Africa." Of course, along with the speaker came a slide presentation that included a picture of all the missionaries in Africa since one of them was usually related to someone in the congregation. This was their way of bringing greetings to those of us in the United States.

The supper itself was a gala affair complete with white paper tablecloths. The Ladies Aid had meticulously planned and re-planned the pot luck to make sure that there would be enough jello salads to go around and that everyone would have plenty to eat. Then there was the family with eight kids that defied established protocol and always brought a can of pork and beans and then made sure they were first in the food line. Once they came with a can of green beans, and everyone thought there had been a complete reassingment of items to bring. Later we found out they had just been late with the chores and had grabbed the first can on the pantry shelf on their way out the door.

Then we got down to the serious business! The program began with the hymn, "I Love to Tell the Story." And when the bulb for the projector had finally been found, the pictures began.

The kids were always positioned in the front row straining to bend their necks back far enough to see the 4 x 4 screen. They always waited with great anticipation the possibility of seeing a "wild animal," but each slide show was like all the others. There was usually a picture of a land rover stuck in a dry creek bed after an unexpected downpour during the dry season, and the closest thing to a wild animal was a dog posed in front of the mission compound.

But the evening had the desired effect on us! After we had sung, "Lost in the Night Do the Heathen Yet Languish," we were convicted to put the old suit coat we had outgrown in the next mission box. Furthermore, we vowed to remember all those starving children in Africa the next time our mothers dared to serve us liver and potato klub.

Another important dinner was held after the harvest was brought in. It was a feast of thanksgiving — but not to be confused with Thanksgiving Day. Ham was served, and blessings were counted. At the end of the meal the offering plate was passed, and we were challenged to "give until it hurts." Some did. Others ate their ham, put in their dollar, and went home.

Next in line was the infamous lutefisk supper held the first Sunday in December. This was one time you certainly didn't want to wait to buy your ticket because each one had a number in the upper right hand corner. This was not there for a drawing; it let you know how long you would have to wait to convert your ticket into that feast fit for a king. If your number was called and you were not present, you would have to wait until everyone had been served before you could eat. That was a chance you didn't want to take!

As it was, those with ticket numbers above 250 were told to go to the sanctuary, take a seat, and begin singing, because the organist would start at the beginning of the black hymnal and work her way through the book. And about every fifteen minutes, the chairman of the Food Line[1] would come up from the basement and shout above the singing, "Vaer sa god," and another fifty people would enthusiastically leave for the dinner.

The scene didn't change much from year to year. We were ushered to a seat, and in no time that jelly-like fish was passed down the long table. Then came the melted butter, mashed potatoes, and the meat balls the Swedes insisted upon. Dessert was fruit soup and these other dieters delights — rommegrot and sweet lefse.

When everyone had been served, the pastor gave his "Mange tusen tak" speech to the committee and gave the chairman a little something for a job well done. Being chairman of the lutefisk dinner had given her special rights and privileges within the rank and file of the congregation. She actually had more say than the president of the congregation — especially during the weeks just prior to the supper.

[1]Chairman of the food line — If she did her job well. she became the leading candidate for next year's overall chairman.

Profits from this most popular of all church suppers were usually designated to go toward something big — a new bell tower or an organ, though people whose ticket numbers had been above 250 always suggested cushions for the church pews.

CHAPTER 17
JELLO

"Pass the JELLO,"
I can still hear it said;
And remember the color
It has to be red!

JELLO

EVERYDAY JELLO

1 small box jello
1 cup hot water
1 cup cold water.

Dissolve jello in hot water. Add cold water and set. This recipe can be doubled.

JELLO FOR A CROWD

4 boxes jello
4 cups hot water.
4 cups cold water.

Dissolve jello in hot water. Be careful to get everything dissolved. Add cold water and refrigerate. When partially set, carefully slice in 1 good sized banana or 2 small. This will feed about 30 people and is good for funerals or other doings. (This recipe was used for the 75th anniversary of the Trinity Lutheran Church).

JELLO STRETCHING

1 box jello
1 cup hot water
1½ cup cold water.

Dissolve jello in hot water. Add cold water and set. This recipe can be used if you need a little bit more jello.

JELLO FOR SILVER WEDDINGS AND OTHER
SPECIAL HOLIDAY DOINGS

3 boxes jello
3 cups hot water
3 cups cold water.

Dissolve jello in hot water. Add cold water and pour into aluminum mold and refrigerate. When partially set, carefully add drained fruit cocktail, bananas, marshmellows or any other favorite ingredients for jello. Before serving, carefully remove from mold and add whipped cream. Serve.

JELLO AND VEGETABLES

1 box jello
1 cup hot water
1 cup cold water.

Dissolve jello in hot water. Add cold water and pour into aluminum mold. Refrigerate. When partially set, carefully add 2 small or 1 large grated carrot, 1 stalk chopped celery. Set till firm. Before serving, carefully remove from mold and serve with salad dressing. This is good for showers.

COMPANY JELLO

1 box red jello (either
  strawberry or cherry)
1 cup hot water
1 cup cold water.

Dissolve jello in hot water. Add cold water and partially set in refrigerator. Slice bananna. (Follow directions for "Jello for a Crowd.") Before serving, top with whipped cream! This is good for Sunday night supper when company drops in.

Footnote: Although there were many flavors of jello, red was by far the most popular. Plain green was used with fish.

Every ethnic group should have a cheer;
The Germans toast, "Hail to our beer!"
Lutefisk and lefse can place the blame
On certain Scandinavians for their fame.

But a little-known food could find a place
In this never-ending battle for first place;
The cry could be heard from the young and the old:
"Time to serve JELLO — take it out of the mold."

Give me a "J" and an "E," double "L" and an "O,"
Come on you Norskies, you're moving too slow.
This is a salad, not a main dish,
Watch so it won't melt into the fish.

Bananas are an added treat
Carefully sliced into the JELLO to eat;
Rise up and be counted as a true Norskie boy,
JELLO is the dish that reminds you of joy.

It giggles and wiggles and bounces around;
It slips off your fork without making a sound;
You can always remember the last call each day:
"Did you all have your fill of JELLO today?"

When relatives came, there was a new treat:
The JELLO was topped with whipped cream — "Let's
    eat!"
"Not so fast," — I felt my hand sting — and it hurt!
"It's no longer salad — now it's dessert!"

So let's give a cheer for that American treat
That all Scandinavians soon learn to eat;
"Pass the JELLO," I can still hear it said;
And remember the color — it has to be red!

CHAPTER 18
GRANDMA'S FAVORITES

Grandma told Mother,
And Mother told me
The secrets of all
The old recipes.

QUICK AND EASY PUNCH

1 package any flavored Kool Aid or Watkins cold drink
1 cup sugar (can substitute honey)
1 tray ice cubes — 12 cubes.

Dissolve sugar and Kool Aid in tap water. Stir well. Add ice. For company add a lemon slice. For silver wedding anniversaries add 1 quart ginger ale to above mixture. Serves 8.

CHICKEN HOT DISH   **Grandma Carlson**

1 large chicken
1 can peas
1 cup diced carrots
1 small onion.

1 cup diced potatoes,
1 cup diced celery
salt and pepper to taste

Cook chicken until done. Bone and dice chicken; use broth to make gravy. Put *all* in layers in a casserole with a sprinkle of flour between layers. Add broth last and a little cream and bake. This one could use this new bought Cream of Chicken soup. This is an old recipe so it could be changed.

MINCED HAM SANDWICH SPREAD FOR DOINGS

1 dozen hard boiled eggs
1½ lb minced ham

onion
salad dressing   (Cont.)

(Cont.)

Grind eggs and minced ham. Add onion and salad dressing to taste. Can be doubled. Another favorite sandwich spread is Cheez Whiz on rye garnished with sliced olives.

LIGHT AND AIRY BUNS

1 c. lukewarm water
2 tsp. sugar
2 pkg. dry yeast
½ c. sugar
½ c. shortening (melted)

3 small tsp. salt
2 T. vinegar
3½ c. lukewarm water
8 to 10 c. flour

Combine water, sugar, and yeast. Let stand about 10 min. Into a large bowl put sugar, shortening, salt, vinegar, water, and flour. Knead real good and let rise twice. Pinch off dough about the size of a crab apple. Place on greased cookie sheets or cake pan. Let rise again. Bake 15 to 20 min. at 400°. Makes about 60 buns. These buns were always served when the new pastor moved into the parsonage.

PRUNE CAKE

½ c. butter
1 c. sugar
2 eggs
1 tsp. cinnamon
1 tsp. vanilla   (Cont.)

½ tsp. cloves
1 c. cut up prunes (cook before) — no juice
1 c. buttermilk with 1 tsp. soda
2 c. sifted cake flour

Cream butter and sugar. Add remaining ingredients. Bake 30 minutes at 350°. Frost with White Icing (recipe elsewhere in chapter) and cut in 4" pieces. Good for funerals.

WHITE ICING

1 cup sugar
½ cup water

2 egg whites beaten stiffly
1 tsp. vanilla

Cook the sugar and water in a small saucepan until it spins a thread. Pour the sugar and water mixture into the beaten egg whites and beat until glossy. Add vanilla and beat again. Spread on cake.

RHUBARD SAUCE

4 cups diced rhubarb
1 c. brown sugar

Small amount of water in bottom of kettle

Put rhubarb, sugar, and water in kettle and cook until tender. This is always a good dessert in the spring and early summer.

CHUNK PICKLES

Wash cucumbers and put in brine whole (Brine is water with salt in enough to float an egg). Soak in brine 3 days. On the 4th day drain off brine water and soak in clear water. On the 5th day cut cucumbers in chunks and put them in a weakened vinegar solution and 1 T. alum. Simmer for 2 hours. Also add green food coloring. After 2 hours drain off water and make brine of 2 cups vinegar, 2 quarts sugar and spices in a bag which consists of 1 oz. stick cinnamon, 1 oz. whole cloves, 1 oz. whole allspice. After it comes to a boil, pour it over the pickles. This is enough brine for a dishpan of pickles. For at least 3 mornings after that, drain off brine and add 1 cup sugar and 1 cup vinegar. After 3rd day put in jars and seal. These pickles go very good with the minced ham spread on buns.

EGG COFFEE

Bring to boil 6 to 7 cups water. Add 3 T. coffee which has been mixed with part of an egg. Boil coffee until the foam disappears being careful so it doesn't cook over. Fill the remainder of the pot with boiling water. To settle the grounds add a bit of cold water.

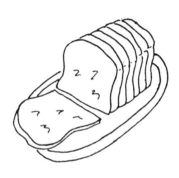

CHAPTER 19
CREAM AND BREAD

We won't make a fuss
To feed all of us;
We'll just have
Cream and Bread!

CREAM AND BREAD

Things were running far behind
One late fall afternoon;
Just coming home from Ladies Aid
I wished it still were June.

The long dark days of winter
Were staring us in the face;
Pa was still out picking corn —
The weather was always a race.

I thought a circus had been brought
Right out there on our farm;
As I drove into the barnyard
I had reason for alarm.

Emil came running from the barn
Hollering, "George is out!"
George was our one and only bull —
Mad without a doubt!

Elsie was high up in a tree
With snorting George below;
I called for help from Uncle Thor,
But he was terribly slow.

We got old George tied to a tree,
Then time to pick those eggs —
Always underneath the clucks
Who wouldn't get up on their legs.

With the cows all milked and the eggs all in,
It was late, so I just said,
"We won't make a fuss to feed all of us,
We'll just have CREAM AND BREAD!"

Reorder Form for *Cream and Bread*

Name _____

Address _____

_____ Zip _____

No. of Copies _____@ $7.95/copy   Subtotal _____

Postage & Handling $2.00   _____

MN Residents add 6.5% sales tax   TOTAL _____

Send cash, check or money order to Redbird Productions, Box 363, Hastings, MN 55033.

For our free brochure and a copy of our new newsletter "MARTIN HOUSE HERALD", send a self addressed stamped envelope to the above address.

If you have not read our second book, *Second Helpings of Cream and Bread*, you can order it from us at Redbird for the price of $7.95 plus postage.

▬ ▪ ▬ ▪ ▬ ▪ ▬ ▪ ▬ ▪ ▬ ▪ ▬ ▪ ▬ ▪ ▬

Reorder Form for *Cream and Bread*

Name _____

Address _____

_____ Zip _____

No. of Copies _____@ $7.95/copy   Subtotal _____

Postage & Handling $2.00   _____

MN Residents add 6.5% sales tax   TOTAL _____

Send cash, check or money order to Redbird Productions, Box 363, Hastings, MN 55033.

For our free brochure and a copy of our new newsletter "MARTIN HOUSE HERALD", send a self addressed stamped envelope to the above address.

If you have not read our second book, *Second Helpings of Cream and Bread*, you can order it from us at Redbird for the price of $7.95 plus postage.

Reorder Form for *Cream and Bread*

Name _____

Address _____

_____ Zip _____

No. of Copies _____@ $7.95/copy   Subtotal _____

Postage & Handling $2.00 _____

MN Residents add 6.5% sales tax   TOTAL _____

Send cash, check or money order to Redbird Productions, Box 363, Hastings, MN 55033.

For our free brochure and a copy of our new newsletter "MARTIN HOUSE HERALD", send a self addressed stamped envelope to the above address.

If you have not read our second book, *Second Helpings of Cream and Bread,* you can order it from us at Redbird for the price of $7.95 plus postage.

━ ■ ━ ■ ━ ■ ━ ■ ━ ■ ━ ■ ━ ■ ━ ■ ━ ■ ━

Reorder Form for *Cream and Bread*

Name _____

Address _____

_____ Zip _____

No. of Copies _____@ $7.95/copy   Subtotal _____

Postage & Handling $2.00 _____

MN Residents add 6.5% sales tax   TOTAL _____

Send cash, check or money order to Redbird Productions, Box 363, Hastings, MN 55033.

For our free brochure and a copy of our new newsletter "MARTIN HOUSE HERALD", send a self addressed stamped envelope to the above address.

If you have not read our second book, *Second Helpings of Cream and Bread,* you can order it from us at Redbird for the price of $7.95 plus postage.